LIVING IN THE WILD: BIG CATS

Anna Claybourne

Chicago, Illinois

Edited by Clare Lewis and Adrian Vigliano
Designed by Tim Bond
Original illustrations © HL Studios
Picture research by Tracy Cummins
Originated by Capstone Global Library Ltd
Printed in CTPS

17 16 15 14 13
10 9 8 7 6 5 4 3 2 1

Library of Congress Cataloging-in-Publication Data

Claybourne, Anna.
  Tigers / Anna Claybourne.
    pages cm. —(Living in the wild–big cats)
  Includes bibliographical references and index.
  ISBN 978-1-4329-8110-5 (hb)—ISBN 978-1-4329-8124-2 (pb) 1.
Tiger—Juvenile literature. I. Title.

  QL737.C23C543 2014
  599.75'5—dc23   2013013023

Acknowledgments

The author and publisher are grateful to the following for permission to reproduce copyright material:
Getty Images pp. 7 (Fuse), 9 (Mark Newman), 10 (Steve Winter), 12 (Visuals Unlimited, Inc./Joe McDonald), 13 (Ary6), 18 (TAO Images Limited), 19 (John Giustina), 20 (Aditya Singh), 35 (British Library/Robana), 39 (National Geographic/Steve Winter), 41 (Theo Allofs); National Geographic p. 27 (MICHAEL NICHOLS); Shutterstock pp. 5 (Volodymyr Burdiak), 15 (Dennis Donohue), 17 (Justin Black), 23 (Ammit Jack), 25 (Eric Gevaert), 28 (Nick Biemans), 33 (rng), 43 (Eric Gevaert), 45 (neelsky); Superstock pp. 22 (Tom Brakefield), 26, 37 (NHPA), 29 (Animals Animals), 31 (Juniors).

Cover photograph of a Bengal tiger reproduced with permission of Getty Images (Mint Images - Frans Lanting).

We would like to thank Michael Bright for his invaluable help in the preparation of this book.

Every effort has been made to contact copyright holders of any material reproduced in this book. Any omissions will be rectified in subsequent printings if notice is given to the publisher.

Disclaimer

Contents

Some words are shown in bold, **like this**. You can find out what they mean by looking in the glossary.

What Are Big Cats?

In the shadows between the trees of an Indian forest, half-hidden in the long, waving grass, a powerful predator lurks. Unseen by a quietly-grazing chital deer, the tiger stealthily creeps closer, crouching low to the ground. A few moments later, it pounces, a flash of orange and black. It leaps onto the chital, its huge jaws clamping around its neck. The tiger's dinner is served.

Furry family

Like small pet cats, tigers, along with other big cats, belong to the cat family, which scientists call the felids. The felid family includes many small and medium-sized cats, such as the Scottish wildcat, lynx, bobcat, and ocelot. Only the biggest members of the family are known as big cats. There are several types, or **species**:

- Tigers
- Lions
- Leopards
- Snow leopards
- Jaguars
- Pumas
- Cheetahs
- Clouded leopards

Being a mammal

Cats are part of a larger animal group, the mammals. Humans are mammals too, and so are dogs, mice, seals and elephants. Mammals all share several features. They have bony skeletons on the inside, and hair or fur on the outside. They are warm-blooded, meaning they can stay warmer than their surroundings. And mother mammals feed their babies on milk from their bodies.

BIG CAT FEATURES

Big cats share several features. Besides being large—at least 5 feet (1.5 meters) long—they are all carnivores or meat-eaters. They are not hunted by other animals, except when they are not yet fully grown. Big cats are also the only cats that can roar, unlike smaller cats, which meow, snarl, or purr.

What Are Tigers?

Of all the big cats living in the wild, the tiger is the biggest. A large male Siberian tiger on all four legs would stand face-to-face with an average 8-year-old human. From nose to tail, he would be almost as long as a small car. He could jump 13–16 feet (4–5 meters) high, higher than a ceiling, or leap up to 30 feet (9 meters) right across a road. A tiger's legs are thick and sturdy, its tail is long and heavy, and its body is packed full of powerful muscles.

Hunting machine

Like other cats, tigers are **predators**, and hunt other animals to eat. A tiger's body is built for leaping suddenly onto large **prey**, like a wild boar or deer, and holding it tight so it cannot escape. However, tigers don't hunt all the time. Like pet cats, they also love to snooze, lounge around, clean themselves and play.

Why do tigers have stripes?

Tigers' bright orange and black stripes make them instantly recognizable to us. However, the stripes actually provide camouflage among the long grasses and leafy forests of Asia, where tigers live. **Camouflage** is vital for tigers, as they hunt their prey by stalking it as quietly and invisibly as possible. Like our fingerprints, each tiger has its own unique pattern of stripes.

Meet the liger

There is one big cat that's bigger than a tiger: the liger. A liger is the offspring of a tiger mother, and a lion father, and can grow to almost 13 feet (4 meters) long. However, ligers only exist in zoos. They aren't really a true species, and are not found in the wild.

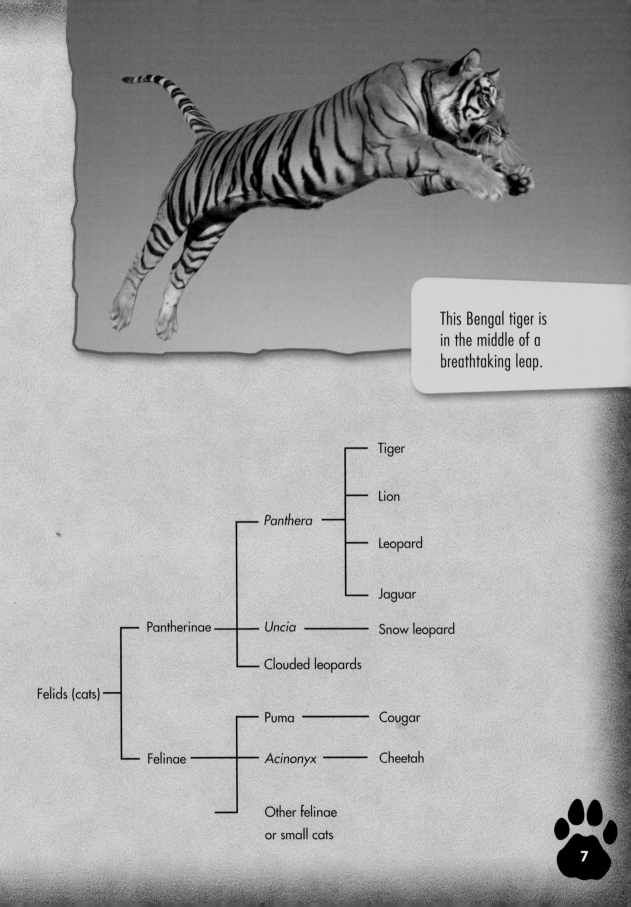

This Bengal tiger is in the middle of a breathtaking leap.

```
                                                    ┌── Tiger
                                                    │
                                                    ├── Lion
                                    ┌── Panthera ───┤
                                    │               ├── Leopard
                                    │               │
                                    │               └── Jaguar
                    ┌── Pantherinae ┤
                    │               ├── Uncia ──────── Snow leopard
                    │               │
                    │               └── Clouded leopards
    Felids (cats) ──┤
                    │               ┌── Puma ────────── Cougar
                    │               │
                    └── Felinae ────┤── Acinonyx ────── Cheetah
                                    │
                                    │
                                    └── Other felinae
                                        or small cats
```

How Are Tigers Classified?

Scientists **classify** all living things, meaning they sort them out into groups to show how they are related. Each species belongs to its own particular group or genus. Each genus belongs to a larger family, each family is part of a larger order, and so on.

Where is the tiger?

A classification triangle like this is a good way to see how a particular animal, such as the tiger, is classified. At the top is the largest group that tigers belong to, the animal kingdom. As you go down, the classification narrows into smaller and smaller groups, such as mammals and cats.

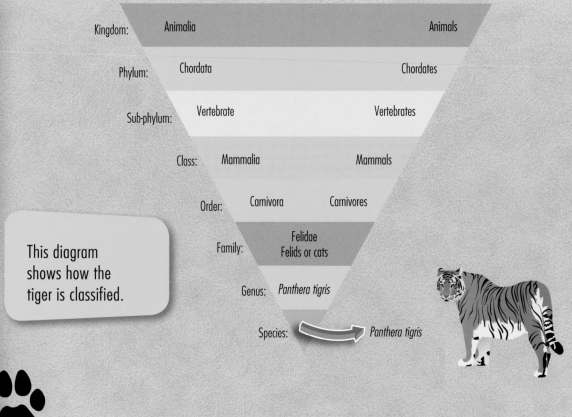

Kingdom:	Animalia	Animals
Phylum:	Chordata	Chordates
Sub-phylum:	Vertebrate	Vertebrates
Class:	Mammalia	Mammals
Order:	Carnivora	Carnivores
Family:	Felidae	Felids or cats
Genus:	Panthera tigris	
Species:	Panthera tigris	

This diagram shows how the tiger is classified.

Six tigers

There is only one species of tiger, but it is divided into six types, or subspecies. The subspecies all look similar, but are different in size and in some body features, such as the thickness and color of their coats. The six subspecies are:

- Siberian or Amur tiger
- Bengal or Indian tiger
- Sumatran tiger
- Indochinese tiger
- South China tiger
- Malayan tiger

There used to be three other subspecies too: the Bali, Javan, and Caspian tigers. They all died out and became **extinct** during the 1900s.

LATIN NAMES

Every living thing has its own scientific name, written in Latin. Scientists all around the world use Latin names so they all know what they are talking about, whatever language they speak. Latin names are always written in italics, and have two parts. The tiger's Latin name is *Panthera tigris*. Subspecies have an extra word added onto the end of their names. For example, the Sumatran tiger is *Panthera tigris sumatrae*.

This is a rare Malayan tiger cub.

Where Do Tigers Live?

A wild Bengal tiger at home in the grassy Indian jungle.

All six living types of tiger are found in southern and eastern parts of Asia. India, Bangladesh, Thailand, Indonesia, and Russia are a few of the countries where you could spot a wild tiger today. However, you would have to be pretty lucky to do so, because wherever they live, tigers are rare.

Who lives where?

As you can see on the map, the different tiger subspecies live in different parts of Asia, and don't usually bump into each other. Sumatran tigers are only found on the island of Sumatra in Indonesia, and Malayan tigers in Malaysia and Singapore. The very rare South China tiger lives in a few parts of China, and the Siberian tiger further north, in chilly Russia. Bengal tigers live mostly in India and Bangladesh, and Indochinese tigers in southeast Asian countries like Thailand and Vietnam.

Past and present

Tigers now mostly live in small areas that are cut off from each other. Long ago, however, they were widespread across most of Asia. The tiger's range, including the Caspian tiger, which is now extinct, once reached almost as far as Europe.

Pacific Ocean

This map shows the past and present ranges of the tiger.

Indian Ocean

Key

■ Indochinese tiger

■ Malayan tiger

■ Sumatran tiger

■ Range of the tiger in the 1800s

■ South China tiger

■ Siberian or Amur tiger

■ Bengal or Indian tiger

Who else lives there?

The place where a tiger lives must also have a healthy **ecosystem**. In an ecosystem, a group of different living things share a living space and feed or rely on each other. A thick forest alone is no good to a tiger. It must have plenty of food species for the tiger to hunt, as well as the plants or other animals that they feed on, and so on.

A Siberian tiger enjoys a roll in the snow.

The tiger's home

Every type of living thing prefers to live in a particular **habitat** or **biome**, the type of surroundings and landscape that suit it best. For a tiger, that usually means forests, thick swamps, or a mixture of trees and long grass. Wherever they live, tigers need cover—plants, bushes or trees that give them plenty of hiding places.

The different tiger subspecies often have slightly different habitats. The Siberian tiger is happy in the snowy, forested landscape of northern Russia, Sumatran tigers prefer thick, hot jungles, and some Bengal tigers make their homes in soggy swamps.

TIGERS IN CAPTIVITY

Many tigers live in **captivity** in zoos and wildlife parks. Shockingly, a huge number of tigers are also kept as pets or show animals. In fact, there are more privately owned "pet" tigers in the U.S. alone, than the total number of tigers living in the wild. There are thought to be fewer than 4,000 wild tigers left.

LOSING HABITAT

One big problem facing tigers is that their natural habitat has shrunk and continues to shrink. Billions of people live in Asia, and they take up a lot of space. Most of the wild, undisturbed land has been replaced with farmland, roads, towns and cities, airports, and factories. Without the habitats and ecosystems they need, tigers can't survive. This is why they have disappeared from so much of Asia.

What Adaptations Help Tigers Survive?

Adapting means changing and becoming more suited to particular surroundings. Animals species gradually **adapt** over time, developing the skills and features that best help them to survive. Animals without adaptations may die out, or move to a different place. In this way, most species end up well-suited to their surroundings and lifestyle.

Tiger bodies

Tigers have many adaptations to help them survive as hunters in their forest, swamp, or grassy habitat. To catch prey to feed themselves, tigers must be strong and fast. They have big, strong bodies with powerful muscles, which allow them to make massive, sudden leaps—the best and fastest way to catch another animal by surprise. Their long tails help them to balance, both when **stalking** and when leaping.

Jaws, paws, and claws

A tiger's mouth and paws are its main weapons, used for grabbing, killing and dragging its prey. A tiger's head is huge, with massive neck and head muscles to give it a powerful bite. Its jaws are so big, it could easily wrap them around your head. Its front legs are especially thick and strong, with very long, sharp claws. When not in use, the claws **retract** into the paws, keeping them sharp and helping the tiger to stalk quietly.

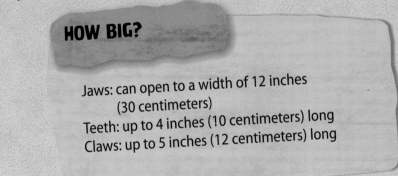

HOW BIG?

Jaws: can open to a width of 12 inches (30 centimeters)

Teeth: up to 4 inches (10 centimeters) long

Claws: up to 5 inches (12 centimeters) long

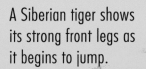

A Siberian tiger shows its strong front legs as it begins to jump.

WARM AND COOL

Tigers live in both hot and cold places. Tigers adapted to cold weather, like the Siberian tiger, have extra-thick fur, which grows even shaggier and warmer in the winter. To cool down, tigers can stick their tongues out and pant, like dogs do. Moisture **evaporates** from the tongue, taking heat out of the body.

Tiger senses

Tigers have excellent senses, which they use to find and catch their food, as well as for communication (see page 28). Several senses come into play as a tiger gets closer to its dinner.

Hearing

When a tiger hears a prey animal nearby, it moves slowly and quietly, so it can listen carefully for the animal's movements. Tigers can swivel their ears around to help them pick up sounds. The tiger stays close to the ground, so the prey doesn't spot it, and tries to stay downwind, so the prey doesn't smell it.

Tiger eyes

As the tiger approach ts vision helps it close in for the kill. Tigers have large eyes with big pupils, to let in as much light as possible when they go hunting by night. Their two eyes face forward like a human's, which gives them **binocular vision**—the ability to judge distances in 3D.

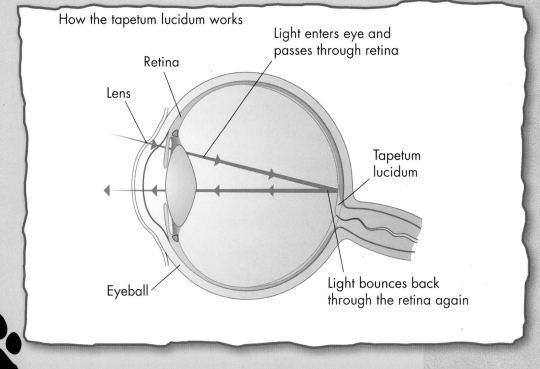

How the tapetum lucidum works

Retina

Lens

Light enters eye and passes through retina

Tapetum lucidum

Eyeball

Light bounces back through the retina again

Tigers have whiskers up to 8 inches (20 centimeters) long all over their muzzles.

Face full of whiskers

Like other cats, tigers have long whiskers which can feel the width of gaps in the dark. Tigers also use their whiskers when leaping on and biting prey. The sensation from the whiskers brushing against the prey helps the tiger to guide its bite to the prey animal's neck and head.

TAPETUM LUCIDUM

Tigers can see about as well as humans in daylight, but much better at night. Like some other animals, they have a shiny, mirror-like layer at the back of each eye, called the **tapetum lucidum**. It reflects light back through the eyeball, so that it hits the retina, the light-sensing part of the eye, twice instead of once.

What Do Tigers Eat?

Tigers are carnivores, meaning they mainly eat meat. Their teeth are shaped for slicing and tearing at raw flesh, and they have very rough tongues which help them to lick and scrape meat from bones.

Favorite foods

If a tiger could choose its next meal, it would probably pick a plump wild pig, or a species of forest deer, such as a chital or sambar. However, tigers have to eat what they can find, and they prey on a wide range of animals, including cows, antelopes, monkeys, lizards, and birds. Sometimes tigers will try to catch the young of larger animals such as elephants; sometimes they will snap up smaller prey such as fish and frogs. A tiger may even help itself to a snack of forest berries or other fruit, though it couldn't survive on them.

Do tigers eat people?

Yes, it can happen, but it's very rare. We are not part of the tiger's normal diet, and most tigers would rather not eat people. However, some do seem to deliberately hunt humans to eat. You can find out more about tiger attacks on page 29.

These two Siberian tigers are eating a freshly caught meal.

TIGERS AND LIVESTOCK

In their wild, natural surroundings, tigers usually hunt wild prey. But if forests are destroyed, tigers can end up running out of their normal prey. When this happens they sometimes start hunting farm animals instead, such as sheep, goats, and cows. This can lead to farmers shooting or poisoning tigers to get rid

It's my lucky day!

Tigers don't kill and eat something every day. Sneaking up on prey doesn't always work, and the animal a tiger is hunting often manages to run away. In fact, scientists think most tigers only manage to kill a large prey animal about once a week. Luckily for them, though, tigers can easily go for a few days without food.

Mine, all mine

The tiger usually drags the prey away and hides it among bushes, or covers it with branches, to keep it secret it from other hungry meat-eaters. Then it comes back every day to feast on the meat until it's all gone. A typical tiger will eat about 45 pounds (20 kilograms) of meat a day, though they can stuff in as much as 65 pounds (30 kilograms).

FEEDING TIME

In zoos, tigers are fed on chunks of meat or whole dead animals. It's too risky for zookeepers to go into the enclosure with the tigers. Instead, they scatter the meat around for the tigers to find, or feed them through the bars using long tongs.

Once a prey animal spots a tiger and runs, it has a good chance of escaping.

Dangerous prey

Some prey will fight back—for example buffaloes slash with their horns and kick with their hooves during a tiger attack. Tigers sometimes die while trying to tackle large prey like these. However, tigers are hardly ever hunted by other meat-eaters, except when they are tiny cubs. They are **apex predators**, and are at the top of the **food chain**. This means they eat other animals, but nothing eats them.

In this **food web**, the arrows point from prey animals to animals that eat them. The tiger is at the top.

Tiger

Gibbon

Loris

Lizards

Wild pig

Elephant

Birds

Insects

Slugs

Deer

Fruit

Nuts

Leaves

Grass

What Is a Tiger's Life Cycle?

Tigers are **solitary** animals—they usually live alone. However, to have babies, a male and female must meet up to mate. They find each other by making loud howling calls that echo through the forest. A male tiger can also tell if a female is around by the smell of her urine on tree trunks and rocks.

Tiger mothers

After mating, the male and female go off on their own again. About 100 days later, the cubs are ready to be born. The mother finds a den, such as a cave or a hidden space under a bush, to have her babies in. There are usually two, three or four cubs in a **litter**.

Cute cubs

Like human babies, newborn tiger cubs are helpless and small—about the size of a pet cat. At first, their eyes are closed. When they open after a few days, they are bright blue, but later change to greenish-gold. For the first two months, the cubs only feed on their mother's milk.

These three young tiger cubs snuggle up to their mother as she looks out for danger.

When they meet up, a male and a female will nuzzle each other, play, and spend time together before mating.

TIGER TERRITORIES

Each tiger has its own **territory**, an area of land that it patrols and guards as its own. Males defend their territories fiercely against other males. But each male territory can overlap with several female ones, so that males and females can meet. A typical male's territory could be 38 square miles (100 square kilometers), the size of a large town. So several territories side by side take up a lot of space. This is one reason why **habitat loss** is a disaster for tigers—it makes it much harder for tigers to

Learning to hunt

From about two months old, the tiger cubs are ready to start eating meat. The mother has to go out hunting to get it, so she leaves the cubs hidden in the den, and brings meat back to them.

At the age of around six months, the cubs start to go with their mother on hunting trips. She teaches them to stalk and pounce on prey, and they practice by stalking flowers, insects, or even each others' tails! Tiger cubs love play-fighting, jumping on each other, and rolling around with their mother.

Tigers have scent glands between their toes that leave a trail on the ground as they walk. The cubs recognize their mother's scent, so they can follow her without getting lost.

Leaving home

By two years old, the cubs are fully grown, and their mother is ready to have a new litter of babies. So the older cubs move away and find their own territories. Male cubs often leave earlier than their sisters, and go on long journeys to set up home far away, while the females usually find a territory close to their mother's.

LIFE OF A TIGER

Gestation period: 90–110 days
Size at birth: 2–4 pounds (1–2 kilograms) and 12–16 inches (30–40 centimeters) long
Start eating meat: 2 months
Start hunting: 6 months
Leave home: 2 years
Start mating and having cubs: 3–4 years
Lifespan: 10–15 years in the wild

These two Sumatran tiger cubs are play-fighting and pouncing on a stick.

CUBS IN DANGER

Some predators, such as leopards, snakes, and wild dogs, may attack and eat small tiger cubs when their mother goes hunting. To keep them as safe as possible, she moves them around to different dens, so that it's harder for predators to learn where the den is.

How Do Tigers Behave?

Tigers are big, fierce, and fast, but a tiger's day-to-day life is actually quite calm. Zookeepers sometimes say that tigers are easy to look after, because they are so relaxed and quiet.

Yaawwn!

If you spotted a tiger in the wild, there's a good chance it would be snoozing or lounging around, and perhaps **grooming** or cleaning itself. Like a pet cat, tigers spend up to 16 hours a day relaxing. They do this to save energy. If they moved around more, they would have to eat more. It's hard work finding enough food, so it makes sense for a tiger to rest a lot.

Tigers love water. They are good swimmers, and often splash around in rivers, swamps, ponds, or even in the ocean. Most tigers live in hot places, and wallowing in water is a great way for them to stay cool.

Hunting time

When twilight comes, tigers become more active and alert. They get up and get ready to go hunting. Tigers are **crepuscular**, meaning they prefer to hunt at dusk and dawn. However, they can hunt at any time of the day or night, if they spot a good chance to catch something.

DR. DALE MIQUELLE AND OLGA

Dr. Dale Miquelle is an American tiger expert who has spent many years with Siberian tigers in Russia. He worked with Olga, a female tiger who had a radio collar fitted to track her movements throughout her life, from 1992 to 2005. She helped experts to find out much more about tiger behavior.

Dale Miquelle at work in Siberia, Russia, measuring a tiger's paw print.

On patrol

Tigers do sometimes move around, mainly to patrol their territories and find food. As a tiger prowls around, it marks trees and rocks with its urine, scat or droppings, and scent from its scent glands. Tigers also leave scratch marks on trees, and roar loudly. To other tigers, all these things show that there's already a tiger territory in the area, and they cannot claim it for themselves.

Get off my land!

Thanks to these signals, tigers usually avoid each other. But sometimes, one tiger will challenge another and try to take over its territory. This can lead to vicious fights, especially between males. The tigers rear up on their hind legs and growl, swipe and scratch at each other. Sometimes, these fights are deadly. More often, the loser will retreat and look for a territory somewhere else.

A male Siberian tiger makes sure his challenger will have the sense to stay away.

In the Sundarbans, people often wear face masks like these on the backs of their heads. Tigers like to sneak up on prey from behind, and the masks are designed to fool them.

Tigers and humans

When tigers come into contact with people, they can be very dangerous. We are not the tiger's main prey, but where farms and towns meet tiger habitat, tiger attacks can happen. In some places, such as the Sundarbans mangrove forests in India and Bangladesh, tigers actually seem to have a taste for humans, and are a serious danger.

JACOBSON'S ORGAN

Tigers don't just smell with their noses. Like some other animals, a tiger has a special smelling organ in the roof of its mouth, called the Jacobson's organ or vomeronasal organ. It's especially good at sniffing out scent messages from other tigers. Tigers and other cats sometimes make a strange grimacing face when they are sucking smells into their mouths for the organ to detect.

A DAY IN THE LIFE OF A BENGAL TIGER

What's a tiger's typical day like? If you were a Bengal tiger, living in the swampy forests of India, it might be a bit like this:

Early morning: Stalking and hunting wild deer, wild boar, or other large prey.

Morning: If the hunt has been a success, it's time to hide the prey somewhere safe, then fill up on food.

Daytime: After a large, meaty meal, a tiger needs a good snooze.

Afternoon: In the hottest part of the day, the tiger may find a cool swamp or river to lie in, and if it's hungry, maybe catch a passing fish as a snack. Males, females, and cubs may sometimes meet up, and relax, play, or bathe together.

Dusk: Time to go hunting again, especially if this morning's hunt wasn't successful.

Nighttime: Often spent prowling around to check on territory, keep scent marks fresh, and look out for prey.

Night shift

Scientists have found that in places where there is a lot of human activity, tigers are more likely to hide during the day and do most of their activities at night, when people are asleep. This makes it easier for humans and tigers to share the same spaces.

A MOTHER'S DAY

A tiger mom with cubs would have a very busy day. She would have to find enough food for the cubs and for herself, teach the cubs to hunt, play with them, and guard them from danger.

How Intelligent Are Tigers?

Tigers aren't on the lists of famously smart animal species, like chimps, crows, and orcas. It's also quite difficult to measure animal intelligence. However, they are thought to be quite clever, at least for a cat.

Tiger learning

One sign of intelligence is the ability to learn. Like many mammals, tigers learn a lot from their parents (for tigers, it's mainly just their mothers) as they grow up. They are also extremely good at learning a "map" of their territory in their minds, including all the pathways around the territory, how far it reaches, where their dens are, and the best places for hunting, meeting a mate, or cooling down in water. Just like a pet cat, they know their way around and how to get home.

Tiger brains

When scientists study animal brains, they don't just measure brain size. They also look at how big an animal's brain is compared to its body, and compared to the average brain size for similar animals. When studying big cat brains, they found that tigers have brains that are much bigger for their body size than other big cats. They seem to be smarter than lions, jaguars, and leopards, even though some of these, such as lions, actually have bigger heads!

Two tigers relax in a zoo enclosure (one of them is a rare white tiger). You can see the strong, high fencing in the background.

ZOO ESCAPES

Tigers seem to be scarily good at escaping from zoo enclosures. A number of zoo tigers have managed to get out by climbing over high fences, or spotting a loose gate latch or a door left open by accident. This has sometimes led to keepers or members of the public being attacked and killed—so zoos have had to make their tiger enclosures even more escape-proof.

What Threats Do Tigers Face?

Tiger are seriously **endangered** (at risk of dying out). There are various reasons for this, but all are caused by humans, and our huge impact on the planet and its wildlife.

Habitat loss

Over the past few hundred years, the human population of Asia has grown, and grown, and grown. Humans have now taken over a huge part of Asia's wild land, destroying forests—the tiger's natural habitat—to make way for cities and farms. Even building a road or railway through a forest can cause problems for tigers. This is because it divides up territories, making it hard for tigers to spread out, meet each other, and mate.

How many tigers?

This chart shows how drastically the number of tigers in the wild has fallen.

1900	Over 100,000
1910	80,000
1970	38,000
1990	
2010	Fewer than 4,000

Game hunting

Game hunting means hunting for sport and fun. Long ago, this kind of hunting was very common, and killing a tiger was seen as especially brave. Tiger hunters would pose proudly beside their dead catch, then have it made into a tiger rug to take home. Not much game hunting happens now, but in the past it was one of the reasons why tiger numbers fell so fast. And, sadly, tigers are still hunted for other reasons (see next page).

A hunting party poses with a dead tiger in this photo taken in India around the year 1900.

JIM CORBETT

Jim Corbett was a famous hunter who lived in India, in the days when it was ruled by Britain. He was so good at shooting that he was often asked to kill tigers and leopards that were attacking local people. He shot dozens of them. Later in his life, though, he turned to conservation, and helped to set up national parks for protecting wildlife.

35

Threats

Today, the threats facing tigers are worse then ever. Besides continued habitat loss, they include **poaching** tigers for their body parts, and hunting to get rid of "problem" tigers.

Poaching for parts

Poaching means hunting that is against the law. There is a worldwide ban on killing tigers and selling their body parts, but it still goes on. Why? The reason is that in some countries, especially China, tiger body parts are thought to have amazing powers as medicines. People pay high prices for medicines made of tiger bone, eyes, whiskers, teeth, claws, and other parts, even though they are banned.

How do they do it?

As poaching is not allowed, poachers work in secret. They set traps or snares, or leave poisoned meat in the forest, then sneak back to see if they have caught a tiger. The body parts are then sold on through chains of illegal dealers and traders, and smuggled around the world.

Tiger fear

Farmers and villagers sometimes shoot tigers that come too close to their homes or farms. They do this to protect local people and farm animals, especially if the tiger has already attacked.

TIGER MEDICINE MYTHS

The beliefs about tiger medicines probably came about because of the tiger's strength and courage. People thought that eating tiger parts might give them similar powers. Yet there is no scientific evidence that any of them work at all.

All six tiger subspecies are at risk, some more than others.

Siberian or Amur tiger	Endangered
Bengal or Indian tiger	Endangered
Sumatran tiger	Critically (very seriously) endangered
Indochinese tiger	Endangered
South China tiger	Critically endangered
Malayan tiger	Endangered

The tiger skin, stuffed tiger cub, and tiger medicine products shown here were seized by police in the UK.

How Can People Help Tigers?

Humans are responsible for the situation tigers are in. But there are several things we can do to try to help them, before it's too late. Lots of people are working hard to save the tiger—and you can help, too.

Save the tiger's home

Like other endangered species, tigers need a safe, natural home most of all. That means conserving and protecting wild forests, along with their ecosystems, so that tigers have somewhere to live, a food supply, and space to spread out and **breed**.

The best way to do this is to create **wildlife reserves** and national parks. These are large areas of land that a country sets aside for wildlife. Inside, no one is allowed to hunt or harm wild animals, or start building, mining or farming on the land. There are now lots of these reserves and parks all over Asia.

Wildlife patrol

Poachers will hunt tigers and other endangered species if they can, even in a protected reserve. So the reserves need **wardens** and guards to patrol them all the time, watching out for danger. They may also have to rescue animals from traps, and sometimes even have fights with poachers. It's a tough job!

Rangers in a national park in India travel around the park by elephant to check up on tigers and other wildlife.

TIGER TEAMS

In some parts of Asia, there are special tiger teams that are allowed to remove tigers to stop them from bothering villagers and farmers. Instead of killing a tiger that is scaring them, locals call the tiger team, who come and catch the tiger, then transport it safely away to a remote forest, far from human dwellings.

Tiger watching

Running wildlife parks costs a lot of money, but one way to get that money back is **eco-tourism**. This means taking paying visitors to see wildlife, without disturbing or harming it. Lots of parks and reserves have places for visitors to stay, tourist paths and guided wildlife-watching tours as a way to make money. This helps local people too, as it gives them good jobs, so they can make a living without doing things like hunting endangered animals.

Tigers in zoos

Zoos help save tigers too, by teaching people about them, and running **captive breeding** programs to help zoo tigers have cubs. Zoos around the world match up and swap male and female tigers so that they can mate and breed, keeping tiger numbers healthy. Visitors flock to see tigers, and especially cubs, raising more money for conservation, and awareness of endangered species.

Big cat charities

There are several wildlife groups and charities that raise money to help tigers. They may also send experts to work protecting or studying wild tigers, and run campaigns to help people understand the problems facing them. Some charities, like WWF and ZSL (the Zoological Society of London), help many kinds of endangered animals. Others, like Panthera, work mainly for tigers and other big cats.

WHAT CAN YOU DO?

- **Adopt a tiger** Many zoos and charities run adoption programs where you pay to help look after a tiger in a zoo or reserve somewhere in the world.

- **Visit the zoo** At a zoo, you can see real tigers up close, while your entrance fee helps to support them. Make sure it's a well-run zoo, though, that contributes to captive breeding programs and conservation campaigns.

- **Do it yourself** If you love tigers, you might even want to become a conservationist, zookeeper, or tiger scientist yourself.

Tourists in a national park in India catch a Bengal tiger on camera.

What Does the Future Hold for Tigers?

Tigers are in serious trouble. Three of the tiger subspecies have already died out, and some others, like the South China tiger, are so rare, they could well die out too.

Which subspecies are strongest?

The Bengal tiger, found mainly in India, is the most common type of tiger. Its numbers are still dropping because of poaching, but if poaching can be stopped, it stands a good chance. The Amur or Siberian tiger, though much rarer, has increased in number thanks to conservation plans—showing that tiger-saving campaigns can work. The Sumatran tiger is also being helped by conservation schemes, and may survive.

The end of tiger poaching

One day soon, tiger poaching will have to stop. That will either happen because tigers die out and disappear, or because we manage to stop the trade in tiger parts. Campaigners hope that people will realize these medicines don't really work before it's too late.

Safe in the zoo

If tigers die out in the wild, there will still be tigers in zoos. It's possible that zoos could keep breeding them, then one day—perhaps if conditions become safer for them—begin to release them back into the wild.

We can all do our part to help wild animals such as tigers.

CHARISMATIC MEGAFAUNA

Conservationists call big, popular animals "charismatic megafauna"—meaning they have a high profile and people like them. Tigers are great examples of this. This is good for them, as it means people are interested in helping them. It's good for the ecosystems where they live too, and the other living things there.

Tiger Profile

Species:	**Bengal tiger**
Latin name:	*Panthera tigris tigris*
Other names:	Royal Bengal tiger, Indian tiger
Length:	8–10 feet (2.5–3 meters)
Weight:	330–550 pounds (120–250 kilograms)
Habitat:	Forests, grasslands, and swamps
Diet:	Deer, wild pigs, cows, bears, and many other animals
Range:	Parts of India, Bangladesh, Nepal, Bhutan, China, and Myanmar
Gestation period:	About 100 days
Number of cubs per litter:	2–5
Life expectancy:	About 15 years

Long, heavy tail helps with balance

Stripes are not just on its fur, but also on its skin

Ears with black and white markings that look like large eyes

Head

Muzzle

Whiskers

Tongue

Long canine teeth for grabbing prey

Legs

Back feet have 4 claws each

Front feet have 5 claws each

Powerful neck muscles

Glossary

adapt to change to suit the surroundings and situation

apex predator hunting animal that is not eaten by other species

binocular vision ability to see in 3D and judge distances, thanks to the slight differences between what the two eyes see

biome type of habitat, such as forests, mountains, or the ocean

breed mate and have babies

camouflage markings or patterns that blend in with the surroundings

captive breeding breeding animals in zoos

captivity somewhere animals are kept, such as a zoo or aquarium

classify to sort into groups

crepuscular active mainly at dawn and dusk

ecosystem habitat and the group of things that live together in it

eco-tourism visiting wild places as a tourist to see wildlife

endangered at risk of dying out and becoming extinct

evaporate to change from a liquid into a gas

extinct no longer existing

food chain sequence in which one creature eats another, which eats another, and so on

food web network of intertwined food chains

grooming cleaning and tidying an animal's coat

habitat natural surroundings that a species lives in

habitat loss disappearance of natural habitat

litter group of baby animals all born to one mother at the same time

poaching hunting animals that are protected by law and shouldn't be hunted

predator living thing that hunts and eats other living things

prey living things that are eaten by other living things

retract to shrink back

solitary preferring to live alone

species particular type of living thing

stalk to creep up slowly and secretly on prey

tapetum lucidum silvery layer at the back of some animals' eyes

territory area that an animal guards and protects as its own

warden someone who patrols and guards a national park

wildlife reserve protected area of land where wildlife can live safely

Find Out More

Books

Carney, Elizabeth. *Everything Big Cats: Pictures to Purr About and Info to Make You Roar!* Des Moines, Iowa:
National Geographic Society, 2011.

Polydoros, Lori. *Tigers: On the Hunt.* Mankato, Minn.:
Capstone Press, 2010.

Portman, Michael. *Tigers in Danger.* New York:
Gareth Stevens Publishing, 2011.

Websites

www.arkive.org/tiger/panthera-tigris
Check out an amazing selection of videos and photos at this site.

kids.nationalgeographic.com/kids/animals/creaturefeature/tiger
This site is full of great information about tigers.

www,nationalzoo.si.edu/animals/greatcats/default.cfm
Keep track of the tigers and other big cats at the Smithsonian National Zoo, and sign up to watch them live via webcams.

Organizations

These organizations are working in various ways to save the tiger. Visit their websites to find out about what's being done, join a campaign or make a donation, or adopt a tiger.

The Zoological Society of London
www.zsl.org/conservation/species/mammals/tiger-conservation

The World Wildlife Fund
www.panda.org/what_we_do/endangered_species/tigers

Panthera
www.panthera.org/species/tiger

Index